THE
RBG
WORKOUT

BRYANT JOHNSON

Illustrations by Patrick Welsh

Houghton Mifflin Harcourt
Boston   New York

Copyright © 2017 by Bryant Johnson
Illustrations © 2017 by Patrick Welsh
Badge and gavel illustrations © Decorwithme/Shutterstock.com

All rights reserved

For information about permission to reproduce selections from this book, write
to trade.permissions@hmhco.com or to Permissions, Houghton Mifflin Harcourt
Publishing Company, 3 Park Avenue, 19th Floor, New York, New York 10016.

Always consult your physician before beginning any exercise program.
This general information is not intended to diagnose any medical condition
or to replace the advice of a healthcare professional.

This book is based on an article by Ben Schreckinger that originally appeared in
POLITICO magazine.

hmhco.com

Library of Congress Cataloging-in-Publication Data is available.
ISBN 978-1-328-91912-0 (hbk)
ISBN 978-1-328-91914-4 (ebk)

Book design by Rachel Newborn

Printed in Canada
FS 10 9 8 7
4500762227

CONTENTS

FOREWORD

In 1999, I had a long bout with colorectal cancer. When surgery, chemotherapy, and radiation were at last done, my ever-supportive spouse insisted, "You look like an Auschwitz survivor. You must get a personal trainer to regain strength and well-being." I asked around, and the United States District Judge for the District of Columbia, Gladys Kessler, recommended Bryant Johnson. Bryant worked in the District Court's Clerk's Office when he was not called away for military service. In his spare time, he pursued an enterprise, Body Justice. Bryant had trained several District Court judges, and all agreed he would be just right for me. That prediction proved entirely correct. At a pace I could manage, Bryant restored my energy as I worked my way back to good health.

Ten years later, in 2009, another challenge confronted me. The diagnosis: pancreatic cancer. Surgery once again and follow-up treatment, leaving me in frail condition. As soon as I could, I resumed workouts with Bryant. Step by step, Bryant restored my energy, adding planks as well as push-ups to my regimen.

I am often consumed by the heavy lifting Supreme Court judging entails, reluctant to cease work until I am sure I've got it right. But when time comes to meet with Bryant, I leave off and join him at the gym for justices. The hour-long routine he has developed suits me to a T. This book, I hope, will help others to experience, as I have, renewed energy to carry on with their work and days.

Ruth Bader Ginsburg
July 24, 2017

INTRODUCTION

When word about Justice Ginsburg's workout got out, people went so crazy for it that I was approached to put it in a book so all of you could do it for yourselves. This opportunity had me humbled, excited, and nervous all at the same time because writing a book was way out of my comfort zone. I wasn't sure how to approach it, which I guess must be how many of my clients feel just before their first training session with me. What I did know was that the first person I needed to discuss this with was Justice Ginsburg herself—if she wasn't okay with it, then the idea for this book would amount to absolutely nothing. Needless to say, she approved the project and you're reading the result.

I've been honing the workout I do with her for the past eighteen years. It's excellent for older people who want to maintain a full life, but it's also challenging enough to leave some of you young ThunderCats panting. (If you're not old enough to know what a ThunderCat is, you probably are one, and I'm just dating myself.)

Let me start by explaining how the workout came to be.

I was born in the city of Newark, New Jersey, but raised in the countryside of Warsaw, Virginia, population 1,500. Now, people love to cook in the country, and I love to eat. As a young boy, eating all that good country cooking wasn't a problem because I was running around playing outside. However, once I graduated high school, it didn't take long for me to figure out that if I wanted to eat what I wanted, whenever I wanted, I'd better start working out. Though I have since evolved from that way of thinking, that was my mindset at the time, and since I was a paratrooper (yes, jumping out of an airplane or helicopter for no reason), I figured I needed to keep my body in shape. But the most important reason was my Aunt Idabell's pound cake, and if you ever tried it, I'm sure you'd understand.

Then, on a whim back in the nineties, I took things to the next level and got certified as a personal trainer. I soon found I didn't have to look far beyond my day job at the U.S. District Court to find clients. I began working with courthouse staff, deputy U.S. marshals, and federal judges. Now, any judge should be familiar with the Latin term *habeas corpus*—literally, "you have the body." However, many of them still needed to be reminded that YOU have a body, and in order for it to take care of you, you have to take care it.

So, that's what I told them, and word of my workout got around. In 1999, when Justice Ginsburg was recovering from cancer and her late husband, Martin, urged her to find a personal trainer, she found me. At the time, she couldn't have done the workout that is now her regular routine, but she was determined as all get-out, and we started building her regimen from scratch.

Justice Ginsburg receives bone density scans every other year. After some years of twice-weekly workouts, her bone density began to increase. The result of this test became my report card for whether the exercises we did were effective or not. My efforts were confirmed by a majority decision when her doctor delivered his verdict: "I'm not sure what you're doing, but keep doing it. It's working."

Keep doing it we have. Other than a deployment in Kuwait from 2004 to 2007 (I deployed—the justice kept doing her important work on the court), we've continued the regimen, and as she's gone from her sixties to her eighties, she keeps getting better at it. We aim to complete the workout twice a week, usually at the gym at the

Supreme Court Building. Sometimes Justice Ginsburg and I chat, but mostly we just get down to it. We usually listen to *PBS NewsHour* while we work, and she always gives it her all. For example, she's graduated from doing push-ups against a wall, to push-ups on her knees, to full-on standard push-ups the way I learned to do them in basic training for the Army. In fact, she's gotten so strong that we've recently added planks to her routine.

Her determination has been inspiring, and she is a living example of what she stands for, including the fight for equal rights for women. She's a strong woman, and in my life I've had plenty of experience with that. My grandmother went deaf at an early age but she never learned sign language, so we communicated through lip reading and charades, a skill that comes in handy when I'm teaching a kickboxing class with the music turned up to eleven. My mother, aunts, and sisters are all strong women, too, so it's no surprise that the justice and I get along so well. As her muscles have gotten stronger, so has our bond. She recently told an audience at Stanford University that I am one of the most important people in her life, and she's had an impact on the most important people in mine.

My niece Cydney was eight when she first met the justice, right after one of our workouts. She's in high school now, and when she came to town this spring to tour colleges, she visited the justice in her chambers. The first time they met, Justice Ginsburg was the taller of the two, and now Cydney towers over her. Meeting the justice, who reached so many "firsts" on her journey to the Supreme Court, is just about the best inspiration for a young woman starting her own higher education.

And you don't have to be young to take inspiration from the justice—just ask my mother. She was interested in the progress the justice had made working out with me, but didn't make the leap to working out herself. Finally, I told her, "Ma, I love you dearly, but I can't care more about you than you care about yourself." She took that to heart. My mother was sixty-nine at the time, and now she's seventy-five and hooked on exercise. She eats more healthfully, too, first becoming a vegetarian and now a vegan, and she's lost about fifty pounds over the years—talk about tipping the scales of justice! She even defeated my sister and a few of her friends who are half her age in a Fitbit challenge, which is no small feat out in the Virginia countryside. My aunts were inspired, too. Aunt Fannie asked me to show her how to use weights for her morning visits to the YMCA, and Aunt Idabell (the baker of the pound cake) walks two miles on the treadmill every morning. My aunts Mary, Betty, and Ethel also make a point of doing some form of exercise several days a week.

I've got the same message for all of you: Whatever you do, *do something.* Whether you're a Supreme Court justice, a clerk, or a janitor, exercise is the great equalizer. A push-up, a squat, a lunge, or a plank doesn't care who you support or don't support. It doesn't care about your race, religion, color, gender, national origin, or sexual orientation. You may have a lifetime appointment to the most powerful job in the world, but your body will still have veto power over you. And you're the only one with jurisdiction over your body, so if you don't use it, you will lose it.

In this book, I present the workout exactly as I do it with Justice Ginsburg, along with some variations for your skill level, personal preferences, and the equipment you've got at hand. If you belong to a gym, do this workout there. If you don't, here's what you'll need to do it at home.

GETTING STARTED

Wear loose, comfortable clothing that you can maneuver in. It can be any synthetic material made for exercise or just a simple cotton T-shirt and gym shorts or pants. (Fortunately for Justice Ginsburg, law schools and all sorts of other places are always giving her free T-shirts, so she always has something to work out in. She also sports a crewneck sweatshirt that says "Super Diva.")

Dumbbells. I recommend having these in a range of weights, from 5 to 20 pounds; you'll need two of each for some of the exercises in this book. As you continue to do the workout and get stronger, you can increase the weight used for each exercise.

Resistance bands and/or resistance tubes. These are essentially interchangeable, though many clients find the tubes easier to use because they have handles. Bands and tubes come in different colors that indicate their resistance level. Buy a few different colors so that you can customize the level of resistance for each exercise.

Door anchor. To do some of the exercises at home, you'll need to thread your resistance band or tube between a door and the door frame. The anchor, which costs five to ten dollars, will help you keep the band or cable in place during those exercises.

BOSU ball. This is an inflated rubber hemisphere attached to a rigid base. It looks like a Swiss ball cut in half, and is optional if you're working out at home.

Medicine ball. This is a heavy ball, usually 4 to 30 pounds and 14 to 36 inches in diameter. You can substitute a gallon-size bottle of water or a large can of peas, anything that has some weight. You can even put some dirt in a plastic bag or use luggage the size of a carry-on bag.

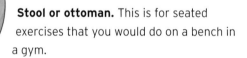

Swiss ball. Also known as an exercise ball or stability ball, this is made of elastic and has a diameter of 14 to 34 inches.

Stool or ottoman. This is for seated exercises that you would do on a bench in a gym.

PRECAUTIONS

Common sense: If it were that common, everybody would have it. That's what my grandmother used to tell me. But do always use your best judgment when it comes to trying new things with your body.

Consult with a doctor before embarking on a new exercise regimen. You can even bring this book and review it with your doctor to be sure it will be right for you. If possible, try the routine with a personal trainer or an experienced workout buddy who can give you tips on form and make sure you're not overexerting yourself.

My clients know I have their best interests at heart, and sometimes I have to protect them from themselves. Justice Ginsburg is very strong-willed and can be determined to get through a workout even if she's injured, so I'll have to adjust the training session. I won't be there while you're working out, so keep an eye out for yourself.

Remember, it took Justice Ginsburg years to perfect this routine—even some young ThunderCats can't complete this workout on their first try. As you first attempt this workout, don't expect to be able to complete it quickly, easily, or even at all. And if you reach a point where you feel like you just caught a ride on the struggle bus and might pass out, pull a muscle, or otherwise hurt yourself, I hereby order you to recuse yourself from the rest of the workout and rest up until you're back at full strength—and then try it again.

WARM-UP

5 MINUTES

Jog or walk at a moderate pace on a treadmill. You can also use a stationary bike, an elliptical trainer, or a rowing machine—whatever you prefer for a short warm-up.

AT-HOME ALTERNATIVES

Do jumping jacks or jog, run, walk, or march in place.

STRETCHES

Think of your muscles as taffy. If you take it out of the refrigerator and try to stretch it, taffy will break. But if you leave taffy out in the sun to warm up, you can stretch it without breaking it. That's why we warm up before we stretch.

NECK ROTATION

3 ROTATIONS IN EACH DIRECTION

Gently rotate your head in a full circle clockwise, then change directions.

Alternative: Turn your head and look to the left, hold for 5 to 10 seconds, then turn to the right and hold for 5 to 10 seconds. Next, look up and hold for 5 to 10 seconds, then look down and hold for 5 to 10 seconds.

ARM & SHOULDER
ROTATION

3 ROTATIONS IN EACH DIRECTION

1. **Stand up straight,** feet spread apart slightly wider than hip-width and arms out like a T, forming a 90-degree angle with your torso.

2. **Slowly move your arms** to make circles a foot in diameter. Rotate to the front 3 times and then rotate to the back 3 times.

HIP ROTATION

3 ROTATIONS IN EACH DIRECTION

1. **Stand up straight** with your feet hip-width apart and your hands on your hips.

2. **Rotate your hips** as if Hula-Hooping in slow motion.

"MAKE LIKE YOU'VE GOT A HULA-HOOP"

LEGS-TOGETHER
KNEES
ROTATION

3 ROTATiONS
iN EaCH
DiRECTiON

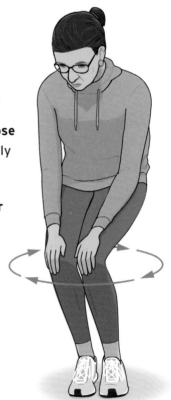

1. **Bring your feet together.**
   Lean forward and place your
   hands on the tops of your
   knees with your buttocks out.

2. **Make sure your knees are close
   together** and draw in your belly
   button.

3. **Use your hands to guide your
   knees in small circles** in one
   direction, then reverse
   direction after 3 rotations.

ANKLE ROTATION

1. **Stand straight with both feet** securely planted.

2. **Raise one foot off the floor** and rotate your ankle clockwise, reversing direction after 3 rotations.

3. **Switch feet** and repeat.

TIP: IF NECESSARY, GRAB ON TO SOMETHING STURDY TO HELP YOU BALANCE.

OVERHEAD ARM STRETCH

1. **Standing straight,** lift your left arm above your head.

2. **Bend your arm to create a V shape,** with your forearm as close as possible to your bicep and upper arm.

3. **With your right hand,** grasp your left elbow.

4. **Gently pull your elbow in and down** toward your head for 10 to 20 seconds.

5. **Repeat** with your other arm.

NECK & SHOULDER
STRETCH

1. **Stand straight** with your feet shoulder-width apart. Extend your arms behind your back.

2. **Grasp your left wrist with your right hand.** Gently pull your left arm down and to the right with your right hand. At the same time, stretch your head toward the right, holding for 10 to 20 seconds.

3. **Repeat** with your other arm.

ON VARIETY

As my grandmother used to say, "A mighty poor mole is a mole who only has one hole to go into." Translation: You've got to have options, and as it is in life, so it is in fitness. When you are in a commercial gym, there are several machines that work the same muscle groups. If you're unsure what machines work a particular muscle group, ask a qualified instructor or gym employee for assistance. If you find that a machine is uncomfortable or becomes boring, try a different one that works the same muscle. This is why I occasionally suggest alternative exercises and methods in this book, especially for those of you working out at home.

UPPER BACK STRETCH & STANDING ABDOMINAL STRETCH

1. **Stand straight** with your feet shoulder-width apart.

2. **Stretch your arms out in front of you,** wrists bent and palms facing away from your body, and interlace your fingers together.

EXERCISE CONTINUES

3. **Reach forward,** keeping your arms at a 90-degree angle with your torso straight. As you stretch, put a hump in your back and attempt to push your belly button toward your back. Hold for 10 to 20 seconds.

4. **From the Upper Back Stretch,** raise your hands above your head, palms facing the sky. Hold for 10 to 20 seconds.

5. **Lean gently left** and hold for 10 to 20 seconds. Lean gently right and hold again.

ON SLEEP

The justice is a cyborg; she's a machine. Some nights she sleeps, some nights she doesn't. I used to suggest that she should get more, but once during our workout, *NewsHour* aired a segment about Ben Franklin that mentioned he slept only four hours a night. We just looked at each other and, though no words were exchanged, the suggestion that she should get more sleep has been stricken from the record. However, most of us need plenty of sleep, so don't shortchange yourself.

TIP: DON'T FORGET TO BREATHE!

STANDING QUAD OR
THIGH STRETCH

1. **Stand straight and stare at a point in front of you.** Raise your right leg behind you and grab your right foot with your right hand.

2. **Pull your right heel toward your buttock** to stretch your thigh. Or pull forward with your quad muscle so that if you were to let go with your hand, your leg would swing forward (but don't let go). Hold for 10 to 20 seconds. Repeat with your left leg.

Tip: If necessary, grab on to something sturdy to help you balance.

GROIN STRETCH (BUTTERFLY)

1. **Sit on the floor,** your back straight and tall, and bend your legs to bring your feet together so the bottoms are touching.

2. **Using your elbows,** gently push your thighs down toward the floor. Hold for 10 to 20 seconds.

SEATED HAMSTRING STRETCH

PART 1

1. **Sit on the floor** and extend your right leg in front of you. Bend your left leg so your foot is against the inner thigh of your extended leg.

2. **Lean forward, bending at your hips.** Extend your arms toward your ankle until you feel a strong stretch in the back of your thigh.

3. **Hold for 10 to 20 seconds.** Repeat on the opposite side.

PART 2

4. **Remain on the floor and extend your legs** out in front of you in opposite directions so that they form a V.

5. **Pivot from your hips** to face your right leg and lean forward. Extend your arms toward your ankle until you feel a strong stretch in the back of your right thigh.

6. **Hold for 10 to 20 seconds.** Repeat on the opposite side.

EXERCISE CONTINUES

TIP: I KNOW A LOT OF GUYS WHO CAN BENCH HUNDREDS OF POUNDS BUT CANNOT DO THIS STRETCH. BUT IT'S AN IMPORTANT PART OF AN OVERALL FITNESS PROGRAM, SO DON'T SKIP IT!

PART 3

7. **Remain on the floor** with your legs extended in opposite directions.

8. **Lean toward the center** of the V made by your legs. Reach forward and hold your arms straight out in front of you. Hold for 10 to 20 seconds.

LOWER BACK STRETCH

1. **Sit on the floor with your legs extended** in front of you.

2. **Bend your right knee up and over** your outstretched left leg, placing your right heel on the floor snug against your outer left thigh.

3. **Extend your left arm,** place it against the outside of your right knee, and press your knee toward your chest, twisting your torso so you're looking over your right shoulder.

4. **Hold for 10 to 20 seconds.** Repeat with your left leg.

CALF STRETCH

1. **Stand facing a wall,** about arm's length away. Step back with your right foot so that it is 2 to 3 feet behind your left foot, keeping your feet flat on the floor.

2. **Lean your body forward** and place your hands against the wall, keeping your head, hips, and heels in one straight line. Try to keep your heels grounded to the floor.

3. **Hold for 10 to 20 seconds.** Switch the position of your legs and repeat.

STRENGTH EXERCISES

When using a machine for the first time, use a very light weight to get a feel for how the machine works. Then you can add weight in small amounts (it is safer to add weight in increments than to start with too much and risk injury). The first couple of weeks with a new client, for each exercise I have them do 2 sets of 12 to 15 reps each. The third week I increase the sets to 3 and decrease the rep count to 10 to 12.

When selecting what weight to start with, if 10 to 12 reps is your goal, pick a weight that will allow you to do 8 good reps with some struggle for the last 2 to 4 reps, while maintaining good form.

When I select the number of reps for my clients, I think about what each person wants to achieve. If you are looking to build muscle, strength, and power—depending on your fitness level—I recommend a heavy weight and 6 to 8 reps. If you want a combination of strength gain and maintenance, I recommend moderate to heavy weights and 10 to 12 reps. If you are looking to increase endurance, use a light weight and do 12 to 15 reps.

SEATED CHEST PRESS (WITH CABLE MACHINE)

3 SETS/10-12 REPS

1. **Sit with your back against the backrest** of the machine with your feet flat on the floor.

2. **Grab the handles and press them forward,** extending your arms until they are straight. Exhale.

3. **Pause for 1 second,** then slowly return to starting position and repeat.

TIP: WHEN USING MACHINES WITH ADJUSTABLE RESISTANCE, BEGIN USING VERY LOW RESISTANCE AND WORK YOUR WAY UP OVER THE COURSE OF SEVERAL WORKOUTS.

AT-HOME ALTERNATIVE

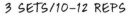

3 SETS/10–12 REPS

1. **Sit on a chair or bench** with a resistance band or tube wrapped behind your upper back, under your armpits, grasping one end of the band in each hand. Bend your arms so that your elbows are against your sides and your hands are close to your chest.

2. **With your hands just below shoulder height,** push straight out until your arms are fully extended, but without locking your elbows.

3. **Return to starting position** and repeat.

(MACHINE) LEG
EXTENSIONS

3 SETS/10-12 REPS

1. **Sit on the machine** so that the foot pad rests just above your ankles.

2. **Extend your legs outward** until they are nearly straight, but without locking your knees.

3. **Return to starting position** with a steady, even motion and repeat.

AT-HOME ALTERNATIVE

1. **Sit on a chair or bench** with a resistance band or tube looped over the front of your right ankle and both ends tucked or wrapped around the back of the chair.

2. **Start with your knee bent at a 90-degree angle** and extend your foot outward until your leg is nearly straight, but without locking your knee.

3. **Return your leg to starting position** and repeat. Repeat with your other leg.

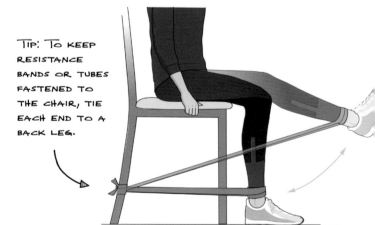

TIP: TO KEEP RESISTANCE BANDS OR TUBES FASTENED TO THE CHAIR, TIE EACH END TO A BACK LEG.

STANDING MACHINE
LEG CURL

3 SETS/
10–12 REPS

1. **Set the machine lever** to the appropriate height for your body. Stand in front of the machine, facing it.

2. **Place the backs of your lower legs against the padded lever,** just a few inches above your ankles and below your calves. Grab the machine's side handles for support.

EXERCISE
CONTINUES

3. **Exhale and curl your leg,** pulling the machine lever as far as possible toward the backs of your thighs. Pause for a second.

4. **Slowly return your leg** to starting position and repeat. Repeat with your other leg.

AT-HOME ALTERNATIVE

3 SETS/10-12 REPS EACH LEG

1. **Stand facing a heavy chair or bench** with one end of a resistance band or tube tied around one ankle and the other end tied around one leg of the chair.

2. **Lift your heel away from the chair** until your knee is bent 90 degrees, with your calves running parallel to the floor. If necessary, hold on to the back of the chair or something else that's sturdy to help you balance.

3. **Slowly return your leg to starting position** and repeat. Repeat with your other leg.

MACHINE PULLDOWNS

3 SETS/12 REPS

1. **Sit on the bench** of the pulldown machine. Grasp the handle with your arms extended fully upward.

2. **Pull the handle down** until it touches your upper chest, bringing the bar under your chin, exhaling as you do.

3. **While inhaling,** slowly return the handle to starting position and repeat.

DON'T FIXATE ON THE NUMBERS

It's not about how much RBG can bench (we don't do bench press, anyhow). It's about making sure she feels good enough to stay on the Supreme Court bench. There's nothing wrong with setting specific goals, but the most important outcome of an exercise routine can't be quantified. It comes down to being healthy, feeling good, and staying consistent.

AT-HOME ALTERNATIVE

3 SETS/10–12 REPS

1. **Slide a resistance band or tube** between an open door and the door frame, toward the top of the door, so that one half is on either side of the door.

2. **Position a chair or bench** so that its center is directly in line with the top of the door.

Tip: When performing these exercises at home, I recommend buying a specially designed anchor (see page 11) that holds the cable in place between the door and the door frame. You can find one for a few bucks online.

3. **Sit facing the door** and grasp an end of the band in each hand, with your hands close together and your arms extended at eye level.

4. **Pull the band down** and in toward your chest, keeping your back straight.

5. **Finish with your hands apart,** close to either side of your torso, just below chest level.

6. **Return** to starting position and repeat.

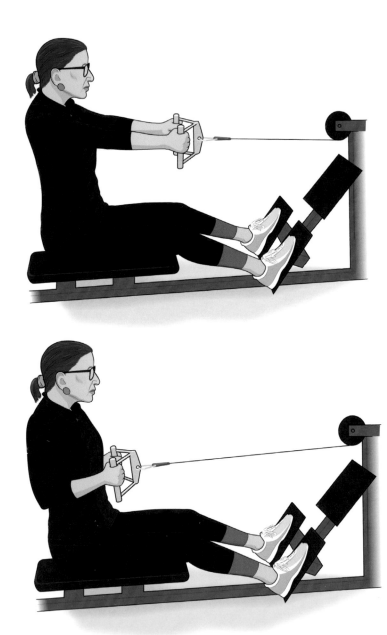

SEATED CABLE ROWS

3 SETS/10–12 REPS

1. **Sit in front of the cable row machine** with your legs slightly bent and your feet placed on the front platform. Hold the V-bar with your palms facing each other and position yourself with your back arched and perpendicular to the bench, your arms nearly straight out in front of you.

2. **Pull the handles back** until your elbows are at a 90-degree angle in front of your torso. Your back should be slightly arched and your chest sticking out.

3. **Slowly return** to starting position and repeat.

AT-HOME ALTERNATIVE

3 SETS/10-12 REPS

1. **Slide a resistance band or tube between an open door and the door frame** at the height of your shoulders while seated.

2. **Position a chair or bench** so that its center is directly in line with the top of the door.

3. **Sit facing the door and grasp the ends of the band** with your hands close together and arms extended slightly below shoulder level.

4. **Keeping your back arched,** pull the ends of the band toward you with your elbows bent and hands apart, close to either side of your torso, level with your solar plexus.

5. **Slowly return** to starting position and repeat.

CHEST FLYS

3 SETS/12 REPS

1. **Adjust the seat height of the machine** so that when you grip the handles, your arms are straight, parallel with the floor, and even with your chest. Keep your shoulders down, chest out, and feet firmly on the floor with your back straight.

2. **Pull your arms forward,** exhaling as you bring the weights around like you're hugging a tree.

3. **Slowly return to starting position,** inhaling as you do, and repeat.

ON FUNNY COUNTING

When I train with Justice Ginsburg, I customize her workout with a bit of "funny counting." If she is going strong,
I'll count her ninth rep as her fifth to push her harder and
get her to do a few extra. If she's fading, I might give her
a break and count her eighth rep as her twelfth and move
her on to the next exercise. Feel free to customize your
own rep counts to match your energy level. There's no
magic number—it's about how the body is responding to
the reps and the intensity that's given to each.

AT-HOME ALTERNATIVE

3 SETS/10–12 REPS

1. **Slide a resistance band or tube** between an open door and the door frame at shoulder height.

2. **Holding on to the ends of the band,** stand facing away from the door with your arms raised on each side of your body, hands just below shoulder level and elbows bent slightly.

3. **Bring your hands together** without bending your elbows further. Imagine you are hugging a barrel or a very large person.

4. **Slowly return** to starting position and repeat.

WORDS TO LIVE BY

> I laugh, I joke, and I have fun, but I'm not playing. I'm serious about what we're doing. The justice also strikes that balance between doing an important job well and having some fun while she does it.

TIP: IN GENERAL, INHALE BEFORE YOU HAVE TO EXERT
THE MOST EFFORT. YOU WANT TO INHALE SO THAT YOUR
MUSCLES HAVE OXYGEN TO GET READY TO PERFORM THE
EXERCISE. THEN EXHALE WHEN YOU ARE EXERTING THE
LEAST EFFORT, USUALLY ON THE RETURN TO THE STARTING
POSITION. OCCASIONALLY I'LL REMIND YOU OF THIS IN
THE EXERCISE INSTRUCTIONS, BUT IT APPLIES TO MOST
STRENGTH-BUILDING EXERCISES.

STANDING
CABLE ROW

3 SETS/12 REPS

1. **Grasp the cable machine handles** with hands close together. Keep your feet shoulder-width apart and your knees slightly bent to relieve stress on your back.

2. **Pull the handles back** toward your torso at chest level. Keep your chest forward and your back straight.

3. **Slowly return** to starting position and repeat.

HOW TO KEEP RBG HAPPY

She's a fan of chocolate, that's for sure, so that's an occasional gift she gets from me. (Never white chocolate, though, because in my book white chocolate isn't real chocolate.) Research even shows that a little high-quality dark chocolate is good for you because it contains powerful disease-fighting antioxidants.

TIP: KEEP YOUR BACK STRAIGHT OR SLIGHTLY ARCHED; DO NOT LEAN BACK OR FORWARD. ENGAGE YOUR CORE, KEEPING YOUR ABS TIGHT. KEEP YOUR CHEST UP AND PINCH YOUR SHOULDER BLADES TOGETHER.

AT-HOME ALTERNATIVE

3 SETS/12 REPS

1. **Slide a resistance band** or tube between an open door and the door frame at chest height.

2. **Grasping the handles,** stand facing the door with your hands close together and arms extended slightly below shoulder level.

3. **Keeping your back arched,** pull the handles toward you. End with your elbows bent and hands apart, close to either side of your torso, level with your solar plexus.

4. **Return to starting position** and repeat.

STAY ON TRACK DURING THE HOLIDAYS

They say "the holidays"; I say, "The holiday is only one day." Eat, enjoy, be merry, then go right back to your routine.

Tip: Do not straighten your arms so far that your elbows lock.

OVERHEAD
TRICEPS PRESS

3 SETS/10–12 REPS

1. **Sit on a chair or bench.**

2. **Holding a dumbbell with both hands** on the top bulb of the weight, start with your arms extended above your head.

3. **Keeping your arms close to your head** and your elbows in, slowly lower the weight behind your head until your forearms are touching your biceps.

4. **Return to starting position** with your arms extended above your head and repeat.

AT-HOME ALTERNATIVE

3 SETS/10–12 REPS

1. **Stand with one foot slightly in front of you** and one foot slightly behind, anchoring a resistance band or tube under your back foot.

2. **Holding one end of the band in each hand,** position your elbows on either side of your head with your arms bent and your hands behind your head.

3. **Raise your arms,** lifting your hands above your head, until your arms are nearly straight.

4. **Return** to starting position and repeat.

ON PROFANITY

When I push my clients to the limit, they blurt out all sorts of things. You can use any four-letter word with me except "can't."

ONE-LEGGED SQUATS

3 SETS/10-12
REPS EACH LEG

1. **Sit on a chair** or bench with your right leg planted on the floor and your left leg raised slightly off the floor.

2. **With one hand**, hold on to the back of another chair or other stable handhold for support.

3. **Stand up off the chair** until your right leg is nearly straight.

4. **Slowly lower yourself back** into the chair and repeat.

5. **Alternate legs** for each set.

TIP: WHEN I DO THIS EXERCISE WITH JUSTICE GINSBURG, SHE HOLDS MY HAND FOR THE SQUAT. IF YOU HAVE A STRONG FRIEND HANDY, GRAB THEIR HAND FOR STABILITY!

HOW DOES RBG DO THIS TWICE A WEEK?

She's TAN (not the color but the acronym): Tough As Nails. And she's had about eighteen years to get good at it. Don't be discouraged if you have to catch the struggle bus with this routine at first, or even for the first few months. Nothing beats a failure but a try.

PUSH-UPS
(REGULAR)

2 SETS/10 REPS

1. **Place your hands flat** on a towel or mat, shoulder-width apart and directly beneath your shoulders. Your legs should be outstretched, with your feet resting on the tips of your toes.

2. **Lower your body** until your elbows are bent to at least a 90-degree angle, keeping your abs flexed and your body in a straight line.

3. **Push back up** to starting position and repeat.

TIP: REST BRIEFLY BETWEEN SETS.

EASIER ALTERNATIVE

2 SETS/10 REPS

1. **Get into push-up position** with your hands flat on the floor directly beneath your shoulders, your knees on the floor, and your ankles crossed. Keep your back and arms straight.

2. **Lower your body** until your belly button touches the floor.

3. **When your chest is 1 inch above the floor,** push back up to starting position and repeat.

The body is like a machine—it's made to move. If you don't move it, you will lose it.

Think of the screw that holds a pair of pliers together. If that screw gets rusty due to inactivity, the pliers will become useless. But if you keep things moving, the screw won't rust and the pliers will remain functional for a very long time.

EASIEST ALTERNATIVE

1. **Stand arm's length away** from a flat wall with your feet spread shoulder-width apart.

2. **Place your palms flat against the wall** at shoulder height and spread shoulder-width apart.

3. **Slowly lean forward,** toward the wall, bending your arms at the elbows.

4. **Straighten your arms** to return to starting position. Exhale as you begin the push from the wall and repeat.

Tip: When I first started training the Justice, she wasn't strong enough to do regular push-ups (she now does 20!), so we began with this easier alternative. If necessary, you can work your way up from push-ups against the wall, to push-ups while resting on your knees, to the full-on regular push-ups.

MEDICINE BALL
PUSH-UPS

1. **Get into push-up position** on your knees on a towel or mat, one foot crossed behind the other, with one hand on the medicine ball and one hand on the floor.

2. **Lower your body until your chest** is 6 to 8 inches from the floor.

3. **Push back up to starting position** and repeat for 10 to 12 reps.

4. **Switch sides and repeat** with your other hand.

DONKEY KICK

3 SETS/10–12 REPS EACH LEG

1. **Position yourself on all fours** on a towel or mat. Your palms should be on the floor, shoulder-width apart, with your knees together, directly beneath your hips, and your feet touching.

2. **Keeping your right knee bent** at a 90-degree angle, flex your right foot as you raise your leg until your knee is level with your hip.

3. **Return to starting position** without touching the floor with your knee and repeat.

4. **Switch sides and repeat** with your other leg.

FIRE HYDRANT

1. **Position yourself on all fours** on a towel or mat. Your palms should be on the floor, shoulder-width apart, with your knees hip-width apart.

2. **Keeping your back straight and your knee bent,** raise your right leg to the side until your thigh is level with the floor. Hold for 1 second.

3. **Slowly return to starting position** and repeat.

4. **Switch sides and repeat** with your other leg.

Tip: To add more resistance to this or the Donkey Kick (page 73), after getting into starting position, place a 3- to 5-pound dumbbell on the back of your leg behind your knee, curl your leg so it grips the dumbbell, and then perform the exercise. Alternatively, use a plastic water bottle or anything else you can hold with the back of your leg. You can also wrap a resistance band or tube around both legs and the heel of the working leg.

ROUNDHOUSE KICK

1 SET/10-12 REPS EaCH LEG

1. **Position yourself on all fours on a towel** or mat. Your palms should be on the floor, shoulder-width apart, with your knees hip-width apart.

2. **Raise one leg to the side** until your thigh is level with the floor, just like in the Fire Hydrant exercise (page 75).

3. **Keeping your leg raised,** kick out to the side, extending your leg until it is straight, but don't lock your knee. Keep your knee as close to your elbow as possible.

4. **Return to starting position** and repeat.

5. **Switch sides and repeat** with your other leg.

TIP: IF YOU'RE DOING THIS EXERCISE CORRECTLY, YOU WILL FEEL A BURNING SENSATION IN THE MIDDLE OF YOUR GLUTEUS MAXIMUS, AKA YOUR BUTTOCKS.

HIP ABDUCTORS

1. **Lie on the right side of your body** on a towel or mat, your right elbow bent, with your head resting on your right palm. Your body should make a straight line from your right elbow to your right heel. Place your left hand on the floor in front of your chest.

2. **Slowly lift your left leg** as high as you can, keeping it straight and your hip extended. Pause when you reach the top.

3. **Slowly lower your leg,** stopping before it touches your right leg. Repeat and switch sides.

TIP: TO ADD MORE RESISTANCE TO HIP ADDUCTORS OR ABDUCTORS, GRASP A DUMBBELL (OR ANYTHING THAT ADDS SOME WEIGHT) AND HOLD IT AGAINST THE OUTSIDE OF YOUR WORKING LEG, OR WRAP A RESISTANCE BAND OR TUBE AROUND BOTH LEGS, AND THEN PERFORM THE EXERCISE.

HIP ADDUCTORS

1. **Lie on the right side of your body** on a towel or mat.

2. **Swing your left leg across your body,** bend your knee, and plant your foot firmly on the floor in front of your right knee. Rest your upper body on your right elbow and keep your right leg straight.

3. **Lift your right leg off the floor** (the range of motion will be small).

4. **Lower your right leg** to starting position, stopping before it touches the floor.

5. **Repeat** and switch sides.

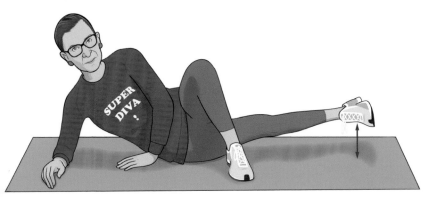

FRONT & SIDE
PLANKS

2 SETS/
30 SECONDS
FRONT

1 SET/
15–30 SECONDS
EaCH SiDE

1. **Assume a push-up-like position** on a towel or mat, with your forearms resting on the floor, your elbows directly beneath your shoulders, and both legs extended.

2. **Hold your body aloft for 30 seconds,** keeping a straight line between your shoulder blades and the backs of your heels. Keep your core tight, and remember to breathe.

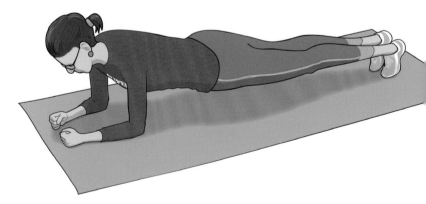

TIP: THEY SAY SOME SUPREME COURT JUSTICES LEAN RIGHT OR LEAN LEFT, BUT I KNOW JUSTICE GINSBURG REMAINS DEAD CENTER—AT LEAST DURING THIS EXERCISE. WHILE SHE IS DOING FRONT PLANKS, I GENTLY NUDGE HER TORSO OFF TO THE SIDE WITH MY LEG (ALTERNATING THE SIDE OF HER BODY THAT I'M STANDING ON), WHICH FORCES HER TO ENGAGE HER CORE TO REMAIN CENTERED. YOU CAN HAVE A FRIEND OR PARTNER DO THE SAME.

3. **Turn onto your right side,** with your right forearm on the floor and your elbow directly beneath your shoulder. Hold your body aloft and raise your left hand straight up toward the ceiling, rest it on your hip, or, if necessary, place it on the floor in front of you until you are strong enough to raise it.

4. **Hold for 15 to 30 seconds** and then switch to your other side and repeat.

5. **Repeat** the front plank hold for 30 seconds.

UPPING THE ANTE

During a recent workout, Justice Ginsburg upped the ante by doing her front plank in a full push-up position, with her hands on the floor, without even realizing she had slipped into this more difficult variation. With enough practice, you may find you want to challenge yourself with the push-up-position variation—or that you've started doing it without even noticing!

SHOULDERS & ARMS ON A BALL

10–12 REPS

1. **Sit on a Swiss ball** with your back straight, chest tall, and core tight. Stabilize your body by planting your feet firmly on the floor.

2. **Grasp a dumbbell** in each hand and hold them by your sides.

TIP: JUSTICE GINSBURG USES 3-POUND DUMBBELLS FOR THIS WORKOUT. YOU CAN USE WHATEVER WORKS BEST FOR YOU, BUT IT'S A GOOD IDEA TO START WITH A LIGHTER WEIGHT UNTIL YOU ARE COMFORTABLE WITH THE EXERCISE.

EXERCISE CONTINUES

NOTE: THE STEPS OF THIS EXERCISE ARE DONE IN ONE CONTINUOUS MOVEMENT.

3. **Slowly raise your arms** to your sides to create a T shape with your torso.

4. **With your arms still raised,** bring them together in front of your face until the dumbbells touch.

5. **Keeping your arms extended,** return them to the sides, creating the T shape again, and then slowly lower to return to starting position and repeat.

SHOULDER
PRESS ON A BALL

2 SETS/10-12 REPS

1. **Sit on a Swiss ball** with your back straight, chest tall, and core tight. Stabilize your body by planting your feet firmly on the floor.

2. **Grasp a dumbbell in each hand** and raise them so that your arms are shoulder height and bent at a 90-degree angle, and your palms are facing forward.

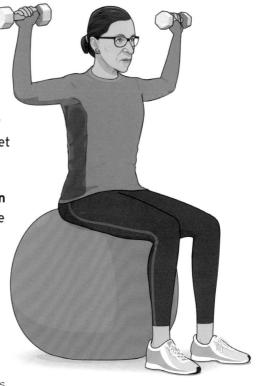

EXERCISE CONTINUES

3. **Raise the dumbbells overhead** until your arms are completely extended and then pause. Slowly lower the dumbbells to return to starting position and repeat.

AT-HOME ALTERNATIVE

1. **Sit on a chair** or Swiss ball.

2. **Hold one end of a resistance band or tube** in each hand while stepping on the middle of the band with your feet.

3. **Perform** the exercise as described.

HORIZONTAL WRIST CURLS
ON A BALL

1 SET/10-12 REPS

1. **Sit on a Swiss ball** with your back straight, chest tall, and core tight. Stabilize your body by planting your feet firmly on the floor.

2. **Grasp a dumbbell** in each hand and hold them with your forearms resting on your thighs. Hold the dumbbells vertically, as though you're holding the sides of a steering wheel.

3. **Slowly curl your wrists** out in opposite directions. Return to starting position and repeat.

TIP: IF YOU DON'T HAVE A SWISS BALL FOR ANY OF THE SITTING EXERCISES, YOU CAN SIT ON A CHAIR OR A BENCH.

PALM-UP WRIST CURLS
ON A BALL

1 SET/10–12 REPS

1. **Sit on a Swiss ball** with your back straight, chest tall, and core tight. Stabilize your body by planting your feet firmly on the floor.

2. **Grasp a dumbbell** in each hand and hold them with your forearms resting on your thighs. Hold the dumbbells horizontally, with your wrists facing up.

3. **Slowly curl your wrists** up toward the ceiling. Return to starting position and repeat.

PALM-DOWN WRIST CURLS
ON A BALL

1. **Sit on a Swiss ball** with your back straight, chest tall, and core tight. Stabilize your body by planting your feet firmly on the floor.

2. **Grasp a dumbbell in each hand** and hold them with your forearms resting on your thighs. Hold the dumbbells horizontally, with your wrists facing down.

3. **Slowly curl your wrists up** toward the ceiling. Return to starting position and repeat.

BACK ROW
ON A BALL

3 SETS/10–12 REPS

1. **Sit on a Swiss ball with your back straight,** chest tall, and core tight. Stabilize your body by planting your feet firmly on the floor.

2. **Grasp a dumbbell in each hand** and bend your arms so that the dumbbells are at ear level and your palms are facing each other, and arch your back slightly.

3. **Extend your arms,** pushing the dumbbells away from your body, until your arms are perpendicular to your torso.

4. **Return to starting position,** arching your back and squeezing as though you are trying to touch your elbows to the middle of your back, and repeat.

AT-HOME ALTERNATIVE

1. **Sit on a Swiss ball** or a chair.

2. **Secure a resistance band or tube** through a door anchor (see page 11) at about eye level and face the anchor point.

3. **Perform the exercise** as described.

 ON WEIGHT

Some women prefer to do only cardiovascular exercise and avoid muscle-building exercises because they do not want to "gain weight" or look big like some of the extreme female bodybuilders. That's the wrong mindset. Building muscle is one of the best ways to avoid putting on fat. And weight-bearing exercises are important for women—especially older women—because they help increase bone density and prevent osteoporosis.

BICEP CURL
WITH SWISS BALL
AGAINST A WALL

3 SETS/
10–12 REPS

1. **Stand and place a Swiss ball** between your lower to mid back and a flat wall. Lean back against the ball at about a 45-degree angle, keeping your spine in a neutral position. Spread your feet shoulder-width apart, with toes pointed forward.

2. **Grasp a dumbbell in each hand** and hold them at your sides, with palms facing in.

3. **Keeping your palms facing inward,** raise the dumbbells to shoulder height, rotating your wrists toward you.

4. **Return to starting position** and repeat.

AT-HOME ALTERNATIVE

1. **Stand or lean** against a flat wall.

2. **Hold one end of a resistance band or tube** in each hand while standing on the middle of the band with your feet.

3. **Perform the exercise** as described.

PORTION CONTROL

What you eat is important, but how much you eat is one of the keys to staying healthy. Try to eat as many fruits, vegetables, lean proteins, and healthy grains as you can, but feel free to indulge in your favorite treats in moderation. And always check the serving size on packaged foods. You may be surprised to find that a bag of fat-free pretzels isn't 110 calories for the whole bag, it's eighteen servings of 110 calories each—which means 1,980 calories per bag. That's over half a pound of fat!

WALL SQUAT
WITH SWISS BALL

3 SETS/10–12 REPS

1. **Stand and place a Swiss ball** between your lower to mid back and a flat wall. Spread your feet shoulder-width apart, with toes pointed forward.

2. **Grasp a dumbbell in each hand** with palms facing in and hold them to your chest, or just let them hang to your sides.

3. **Slowly bend your knees** to a 90-degree angle while inhaling.

4. **Squeeze your buttocks,** straighten your legs, and exhale slowly while returning to starting position, and repeat.

During one workout, we caught a special on *NewsHour* on Justice Ginsburg and Antonin Scalia. No one could understand why they were the best of friends. She looked over at me and said, "He makes me laugh." Isn't it just as simple as that? To have opposing ideas and still be best of friends is what life is really about. It's like the old *Looney Tunes* cartoons with Ralph Wolf and Sam Sheepdog. Oh, you don't remember? I guess I'm dating myself again.

AT-HOME ALTERNATIVE

1. **Stand and lean** against a flat wall.

2. **Hold one end of a resistance band or tube in each hand** while standing on the middle of the band with your feet.

3. **Perform the exercise** as described.

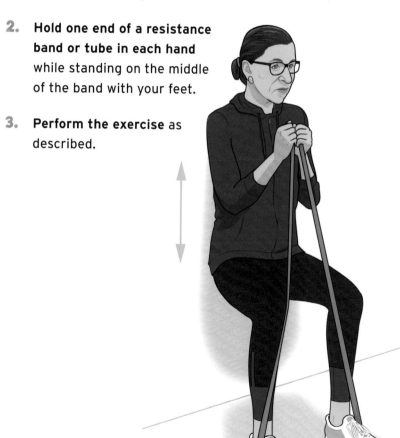

KNEE LIFTS

1 SET/10-12 REPS EACH LEG

1. **Place a step, bench, or sturdy box** in front of you. Step firmly onto it with your right foot while pushing off the floor with your left foot.

2. **As you plant your right foot on the step,** bring up your left knee as high as you can.

3. **Step back onto the floor with both feet** and repeat, alternating the lead foot for each rep.

EATING ADVICE

You eat to live, you don't live to eat. Don't get me wrong, I love to eat—I throw down hard on Thanksgiving and other celebrations. But you should go wild only once in a while, and only if you're balancing it with an active lifestyle.

QUARTER TO HALF SQUAT

3 SETS/10–12 REPS

1. **Hold on to a pole,** door frame, or other stable object with your feet hip-width apart.

2. **With your back straight, bend your knees** and lower yourself to anywhere from a quarter of the way down to about halfway down, or to a full 90-degree squat.

3. **Return to starting position**, pushing up with your glutes, legs, and core, and repeat.

TELLING JOKES TO THE JUSTICE

Sometimes the justice laughs. Sometimes she doesn't. It is still funny to me.

STANDING KNEE RAISES

3 SETS/10–12 REPS EACH LEG

1. **Hold on to a pole, door frame,** or other stable object with one hand, with feet hip-width apart. If necessary for balance, hold the pole with both hands.

2. **Lift your right knee** and bring it as close to your chest as possible, tucking your pelvis as you do. At the same time, crunch your upper body downward and bring your free hand to the knee you are raising. If you're using both hands for balance, just lift and tuck.

3. **Return to starting position** in a controlled motion and repeat on the other side, alternating legs with each rep.

LEG SWINGS

1. **Place both hands on a pole** or wall at waist or shoulder level. Lean into the pole or wall for support.

2. **With a slight bend in your right knee** and your right foot flexed upward, swing your right leg to the right, then across your body to the left.

3. **Repeat** and then switch legs.

THE BALANCE OF POWER

The balance of power is a fundamental principle for any workout regimen. Some people like to work out just their chest and biceps, and they end up with the posture of a gorilla. It's important to perform strength exercises on all major muscle groups. Don't skip the legs!

KNEE LIFT & SWING

1 SET/10–12
SWiNGS EaCH LEG

1. **Place both hands on a pole** or wall at waist or shoulder level.

2. **Raise your right leg in front of you** so that it is bent at a 90-degree angle and your thigh is parallel to the floor.

3. **While keeping your leg raised,** swing it outward and inward from the hip.

4. **Repeat** and then switch legs.

TIP: THIS EXERCISE OPENS AND CLOSES YOUR HIPS, WHICH HELPS INCREASE YOUR RANGE OF MOTION AND IMPROVE CIRCULATION.

SQUAT
ON BOSU BALL

3 SETS/
10 REPS

1. **Stand on the round side of a BOSU ball** with your legs 6 to 8 inches apart, chest up, and eyes forward.

2. **Lower your body, flexing your knees and hips.** Keep your knees aligned with your feet and hips—don't allow them to poke out to the side. Squat as low as your body allows and pause when you reach the bottom of the motion.

3. **Return to starting position** by extending your knees and hips and pushing upward, engaging your quadriceps, and repeat.

TIP: FOR THIS EXERCISE, IF YOU DON'T HAVE A BOSU BALL, YOU CAN DO THE EXERCISE WHILE STANDING ON A CUSHION OR PILLOW, OR DIRECTLY ON THE FLOOR.

BENCH SIT & STAND
WITH MEDICINE BALL

3 SETS/8–10 REPS

I tell Justice Ginsburg this is one of the most important exercises of her entire workout. Why? Because if you can't do it, you also won't be able to get on and off a toilet by yourself, and you'll have to have a nursing attendant 24/7.

1. **Stand with a bench directly behind you,** feet shoulder-width apart and toes turned slightly outward. Hold a medicine ball at your chest, arms extended so they are perpendicular to your body.

2. **Slowly bend your legs and sit down softly** on the bench. As you sit, fold in your arms to bring the ball to your chest.

EXERCISE CONTINUES

3. **Return to starting position** by pushing through your heels and the middles of your feet, extending your arms as you stand, and repeat.

4. **To complete the full version of this exercise,** with each rep, toss the medicine ball to a friend or partner as you stand up, and have them toss or hand it back to you with each rep. If you are alone, just hold the medicine ball at eye level as you complete the reps and extend and bring it back to your chest with each rep.

COOLDOWN

If time and energy level allow, conduct another round of stretches at the end of your workout—this will help bring your heart rate and breathing back to normal. And remember to always pay attention to your body. If you start feeling sharp pains, severe pain, or discomfort, then stop immediately.

Congratulations! You've now completed the same workout that Justice Ginsburg and I do together twice a week. I've watched her make amazing progress over the years, and I know that you can, too, if you stick with it.

Stay strong! And "It All Begins with Attitude."

ACKNOWLEDGMENTS

None of this would have been possible if it were not for the many people who have come in and out of my life in one way or another.

Thank you:

Justice Ginsburg, for having trust and confidence in me all these years. **Kimberly McKenzie** and **Lauren Brewer,** for keeping the schedules straight, along with important and helpful reminders. **Judge Thomas Hogan,** the first of many judges who trusted me to be his personal trainer, and **Judge Gladys Kessler,** who referred me to Justice Ginsburg.

G'Von Brown, my first workout partner and the original "Stuff Knower," you showed me how to train and how to be trained, and **Adrien Mobley,** who suggested I should get certified as a personal trainer.

My courthouse family: Angela Caesar, the current Clerk of Court, who has always supported me; **Tawana Davis,** my first client; **Elizabeth Paret,** my Gemini twin sister, second client, and first unofficial public relations person, who talked me up to anyone who would listen; and **Jenna Gatski,** my second unofficial PR person, who talked me up so much that my story made the front page of the *Washington Post* in 2013.

My military family from the 11th Special Forces Group, 311th and 335th TSC, and the 200th MP Cmd. Fitness is a major part of military life and I have always had the support of my brothers and sisters in arms. **Chief Diane Robinson, Linda Dorsey, Joan Collins, and Amanda Rohr** for supporting me the three years I was deployed in a faraway land.

My International Sports Conditioning Association (ISCA) family: Thomas the Promise, for teaching me the foundation of sports conditioning; **Dwight Smith** and **Dennis Davis,** my ISCA brothers from another mother; **Christine Kwok,** my ISCA "Buddy" and fitness sounding board; **Desire Williams,** for introducing me to **Michael and Irene Blanks,** who showed me how to give your all when teaching a kickboxing class and create an energy that makes your students give more than they knew they could while staying humble. Michael, you also provided me with the hottest music mixes that anyone has ever heard, which allowed me to teach kickboxing classes while deployed and touch many people.

Jonathan Gilbert, my acupuncturist, for keeping my body running when I burn the candle at both ends and in the middle.

Julio and Leneide Boaventura, my Brazilian brother and sister who provided me an opportunity to teach and train in their beautiful country. The language barrier never stopped me from receiving the energy and love and becoming a part of the Brazilian culture and their family. *Muito obrigado tudo beleza.*

Ben Schreckinger, the rider of the struggle bus, for capturing my energy and personality and helping put my words to print—you are good at what you do and I appreciate all your assistance.

My awesome agents **Esther Newberg** and **Zoe Sandler,** you told me you had my back and stayed true to your word. I thank you and hope our relationship continues to grow.

Deborah Brody, Rachel Newborn, and **Jamie Selzer,** you saw the vision of this book and made it a reality. Words cannot express my gratitude for the opportunity you have given me and how you made this process smooth and easy.

Patrick Welsh, for your fantastic illustrations that bring the workout to life on every page.

My classmates from the 1982 class of Rappahannock High School; we were one of the first K-12 integrated classes in Richmond County. The diversity we shared at an early age has provided me the foundation needed to be able to adjust and adapt to the various clients I have trained.

Last, but surely not least, I want to thank **God** and **my always supportive family,** especially the strong women who raised me and taught me to believe in God and to trust the process: my grandmother **Essie Johnson;** my mother, **Dorothy Johnson;** my aunts **Fannie Johnson, Ethel Wood, Idabell Bushrod, Mary Kelly,** and **Betty Batchelor;** my sisters **Christy Johnson** and **Rosalyn Davis.** Also, my grandfather **Albert Johnson;** my father, **Braster Staton, Jr.;** my uncles **Willie (Billy) Johnson, Walter Johnson,** and **Frank Johnson;** and **my many cousins, other family members, and friends I didn't mention.**

My clients: It's always about them. I give them all I have because I am thankful and truly humbled that they trust me to help them to help themselves.

ABOUT THE AUTHOR

Photograph by Abby Greenawalt

Bryant Johnson has worked as a personal trainer for twenty years and has trained Justice Ruth Bader Ginsburg since 1999. He counts among his clients numerous Federal Court justices, judges, attorneys, and clerks, and he has trained military and civilian personnel around the world. Johnson is certified as a personal trainer by the American Council on Exercise (ACE), a master trainer by the International Sports and Conditioning Association (ISCA), and a master fitness trainer by the United States military.

A member of the U.S. Army for over thirty years, twelve of those as a member of a Special Forces Airborne Unit, he is also a graduate of Grantham University and DeVry University. He lives in Washington, D.C.

Photograph by Abby Greenawalt